INSIDE MODERN
CITIES

SUPPLYING WATER
FOR A CITY

BY CECILIA PINTO McCARTHY

CONTENT CONSULTANT
Amy Pruden, PhD
Professor of Civil and Environmental Engineering
Virginia Tech

Core Library

Cover image: Rooftop water towers store water and
deliver it to buildings.

An Imprint of Abdo Publishing
abdopublishing.com

abdopublishing.com

Published by Abdo Publishing, a division of ABDO, PO Box 398166, Minneapolis, Minnesota 55439. Copyright © 2019 by Abdo Consulting Group, Inc. International copyrights reserved in all countries. No part of this book may be reproduced in any form without written permission from the publisher. Core Library™ is a trademark and logo of Abdo Publishing.

Printed in the United States of America, North Mankato, Minnesota
042018
092018

THIS BOOK CONTAINS RECYCLED MATERIALS

Cover Photo: Shutterstock Images
Interior Photos: Shutterstock Images, 1, 10, 24–25, 34 (cloud), 34 (treatment plant), 34 (house); F. Grao/Shutterstock Images, 4–5; Alexandr Kryazhev/Sputnik/AP Images, 7; Jin Ward/ Shutterstock Images, 12–13; Red Line Editorial, 15; iStockphoto, 18, 32–33, 43; Tang Wei/ Imaginechina/AP Images, 20; View Stock Stock Connection USA/Newscom, 22–23, 45; Andrea Izzotti/Shutterstock Images, 29; Redline Vector/iStockphoto, 34 (reservoir); Sovenko Artem/ Shutterstock Images, 34 (storage); Pro Stock Studio/Shutterstock Images, 34 (boat); Maria Bobrova/ Shutterstock Images, 37

Editor: Maddie Spalding
Imprint Designer: Maggie Villaume
Series Design Direction: Claire Vanden Branden

Library of Congress Control Number: 2017962646

Publisher's Cataloging-in-Publication Data

Names: McCarthy, Cecilia Pinto, author.
Title: Supplying water for a city / by Cecilia Pinto McCarthy.
Description: Minneapolis, Minnesota : Abdo Publishing, 2019. | Series: Inside modern cities | Includes online resources and index.
Identifiers: ISBN 9781532114854 (lib.bdg.) | ISBN 9781532154683 (ebook)
Subjects: LCSH: Engineering design--Juvenile literature. | Water-supply engineering-- Juvenile literature. | City planning--Juvenile literature. | Cities and towns--Juvenile literature. | Municipal water supply--Juvenile literature.
Classification: DDC 624.023--dc23

CONTENTS

FROM SOURCE TO FAUCET

Approximately 8.5 million people live in New York City. This makes it the largest US city. Supplying water to all of New York City requires a large water treatment system. Each day, people in New York City use approximately 1 billion gallons (3.8 billion L) of water. The water comes from 19 reservoirs and three controlled lakes. Reservoirs are man-made lakes. These water sources are located north of the city.

The water in a reservoir or controlled lake may contain dangerous microbes. These tiny organisms can make people sick.

A reservoir in New York City's Central Park was built in 1862 and provided water for the city until 1991.

Disinfecting the water makes it safe to use. This process involves adding chlorine or other chemicals to the water. Chlorine is a chemical that kills germs. It also prevents bacteria from growing inside water pipes. Disinfection usually happens inside a treatment plant. But chlorine may be added to water while it's in a reservoir. This is the case in New York's Kensico Reservoir. This reservoir supplies water to parts of the state, including New York City. Fluoride is also added to water in the reservoir. This chemical helps keep teeth healthy. Toothpaste often contains fluoride.

Water from the Kensico Reservoir enters the Catskill-Delaware Water Ultraviolet Disinfection Facility. More than 2.2 billion gallons (8.3 billion L) of water pass through this plant each day. Water flows through a system of pipes into 56 tanks. Inside each tank, special lamps shine ultraviolet (UV) light into the water. UV light is a type of invisible light given off by the sun. This is the type of light that gives people sunburns. Energy from

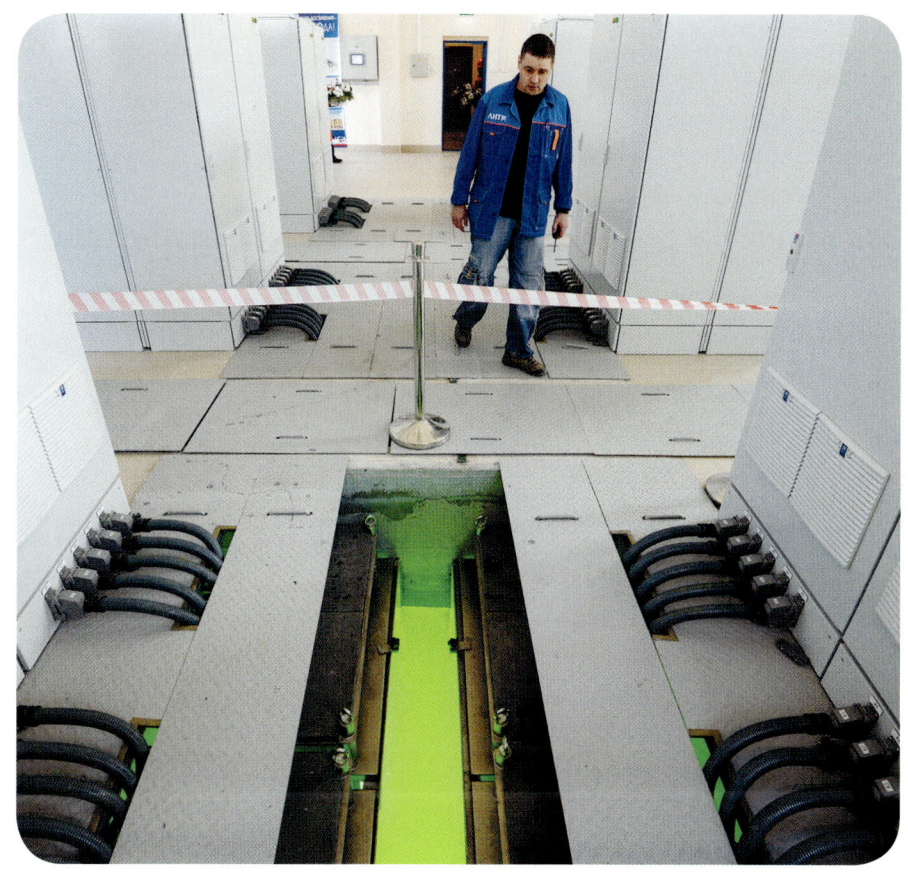

Some water treatment plants add chemicals to disinfect water, but others use ultraviolet light instead.

the light enters microbes in the water. This damages the microbes, making them inactive and harmless.

The Croton Water Filtration Plant also treats some of New York State's water. Chemicals are added that bind to particles in the water. The particles rise to the surface. Then they are removed. The water is

WATER TUNNEL NO. 3

In 1970 construction began on a new water tunnel for New York City. This tunnel will supply water to the city if the city's two older tunnels need to be shut down for repairs. Water Tunnel No. 3 is being built in four stages. Some parts of the tunnel are 800 feet (244 m) below street level. The tunnel will be more than 60 miles (97 km) long when completed. It is one of the most complicated engineering projects in the world. It has also been expensive for the city to finance this project, which led to delays. The tunnel is expected to open in 2020.

treated with UV light. Then it is disinfected with chemicals. This treatment ensures the water is clean and safe.

A CONSTANT FLOW

When people turn on a faucet, they expect to see water that is clean and clear. People need water to drink, bathe, cook, and clean. Water runs machinery and puts out fires. Each day, Americans use approximately 42 billion gallons (159 billion L) of water. The water is delivered to cities and towns through approximately 1 million miles (1.6 million km) of pipes.

Pipes are just one part of the water supply system. Dams, reservoirs, tanks, and treatment plants are also part of this system. Most cities get their water from lakes and rivers. Dams and reservoirs store the water. Water flows from reservoirs through pipes into treatment plants. After the water is treated, it is pumped out of the plant through pipes. The water is held in a storage tank, such as a water tower.

Systems operators at water treatment plants make sure equipment is working well.

From there, the water is pumped through underground pipes. Finally, it reaches homes and businesses.

CREATING A WATER SUPPLY SYSTEM

Many people work together to build and operate water supply systems. Geographic information system (GIS) specialists analyze land and water resources.

They collect data and create maps. Water resource engineers design systems for water storage, collection, and delivery. Hydrologists and hydraulic engineers study how water flows. They assess whether water sources can provide enough water to meet a community's needs. They also test water quality. Other kinds of engineers design dams, pipelines, and pumps. Environmental engineers may plan and design water treatment plants. It takes a team of scientists and engineers to make sure communities have plenty of safe water each day.

EXPLORE ONLINE

Chapter One talks about experts who develop water supply infrastructure. At the website below, an environmental engineer discusses the projects he works on. How is the information in this website the same as the information in Chapter One? What new information did you learn from the website?

ENVIRONMENTAL ENGINEER PROFILE
abdocorelibrary.com/supplying-water

STORING AND MOVING WATER

Approximately 71 percent of Earth's surface is covered in water. As the sun warms the planet, water evaporates and becomes a gas. The gas rises into the atmosphere, where it cools and forms clouds. Then the water returns to Earth as precipitation, such as rain or snow. Some precipitation soaks into the ground. Some falls into rivers, oceans, and other bodies of water. Then it can evaporate again. This continuous movement of water is called the water cycle.

Reservoirs supply cities and surrounding areas with water.

SOURCES OF WATER

More than 96 percent of Earth's water is salt water. Salt water contains large amounts of dissolved salts. Less than 3 percent of the water on Earth is fresh water. Fresh water has low amounts of salt. Fresh water can be treated to become usable water.

Usable water is made up of surface water and groundwater. Water from rivers, streams, and lakes is surface water. Most of the water people use for drinking is surface water. The amount of surface water can vary. After a rainstorm, rivers may overflow with water. At other times, areas may experience a drought. A drought occurs when there is little or no precipitation for a long time. Droughts can cause lakes to shrink or dry up.

Groundwater comes from rain or snow melt that soaks into the soil. The water moves underground and fills up spaces between rocks. Surface water and groundwater together make up an area's watershed. A watershed is an area of land where water flows to a

US WATER USE
TRENDS

This graph shows water usage in the United States from 1950 to 2010. How has water usage changed over the years? What do you think may be the reasons for this change? Based on this trend, how do you think water usage will continue to change?

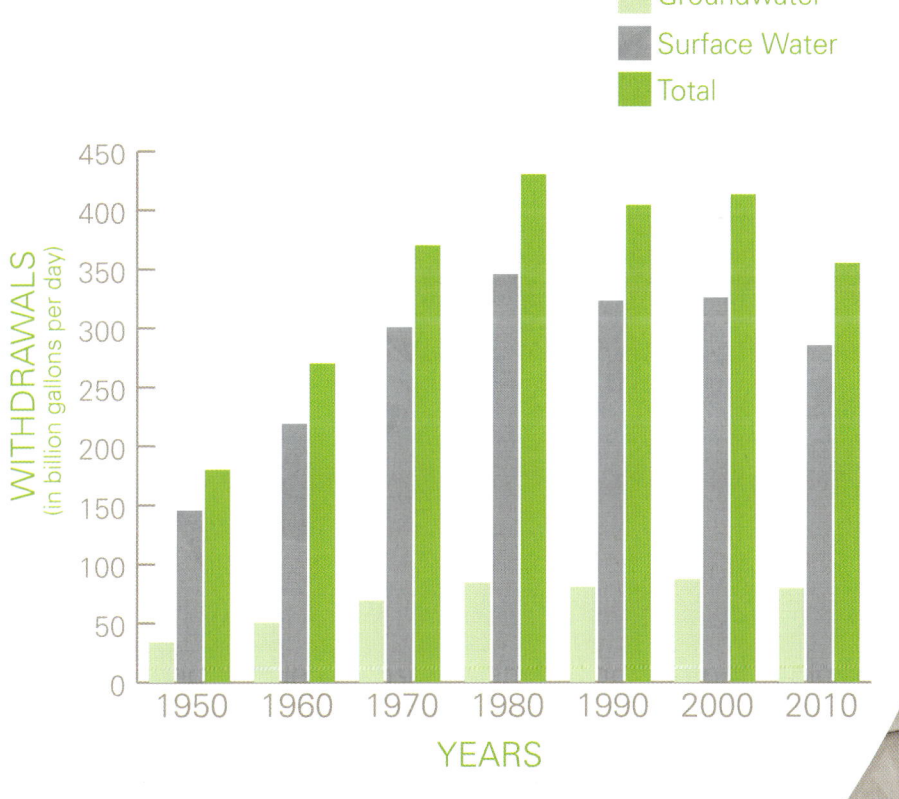

common outlet. This water often flows into a river that empties into an ocean. Communities rely on watersheds for their water.

AQUIFERS AND WELLS

Groundwater can be found in aquifers. An aquifer is an underground layer of rock and sand. People get water from an aquifer by digging or drilling a well into the ground. The water is pumped up to the surface through pipes. Aquifers are refilled by precipitation, such as rain and snow. This process is called recharging. If too much water is pumped out of aquifers, they may run dry.

DAMS AND RESERVOIRS

People also store surface water in reservoirs. Some reservoirs are created by building a dam. Dams are barriers that manage the flow of water. They are usually built across rivers.

Before a dam is built, engineers and scientists study the site. They look at rock and soil samples. The site must be stable enough to support a dam.

Engineers consider whether the area is prone to earthquakes. Scientists examine how the dam may affect wildlife and the environment.

Modern dams are made of either concrete or earth and rock. Dams made of earth and rock are called embankment dams. All dams must be strong enough to resist the force of water pushing against them. Gates in the dam control the amount of water in the reservoir.

ROBOTIC BUOYS

Robotic monitoring buoys are tools that can gather data in a reservoir. These buoys are used in the Ashokan Reservoir in New York. They sit on floating platforms. They are equipped with sensors. The sensors collect information about water quality. Antennas on the buoys transmit this information back to scientists. During winter, the robotic buoys are replaced with under-ice buoys. Under-ice buoys are not damaged in cold conditions. These buoys have a steel cable with sensors. The sensors monitor the water at different depths. This information helps scientists understand how storms and snow affect the quality of the reservoir's water.

Engineers design dams in many ways. The type of dam built in an area depends on the geology of the land. Engineers first create models of dams. The models are tested to see if they can handle water pressure and other stress. Computer programs analyze the results. The outcome shows how a real dam may hold up under the same conditions. If needed,

PERSPECTIVES
ENVIRONMENTAL IMPACTS

Reservoirs and dams can have a negative impact on the environment. Dams built across rivers may prevent fish from migrating to breeding grounds. When rivers are dammed, the temperature and movement of the water changes. Fish and other animals may not be able to adapt to the changes in their habitat. They may struggle to survive. Reservoirs and dams also prevent the natural flow of nutrients downstream. Nutrients help plants and trees grow. As a result, fewer plants and trees may grow around a reservoir. This creates poor soil that may easily wash away.

Dams can be used to contain water in a reservoir.

Pumping stations push water from reservoirs into water treatment plants.

engineers can change the design of the dam before building begins.

Some reservoirs are not made by damming. Some are formed when pipelines or canals direct water from a river to a hollow or low-lying area. Workers line the reservoir with clay. The clay keeps water from seeping into the soil.

MOVING WATER

Water from rivers and streams flows downhill. It travels through aqueducts. Aqueducts may be large underground pipes. They may also be open canals, or waterways. Aqueducts connect to reservoirs.

In a reservoir, water flows through intake pipes. These pipes direct water into a treatment plant. In low-lying areas, a pumping station is used to move water from a reservoir. Inside the station, pumps increase the water pressure. The increased pressure forces the water through a pipeline into a water treatment plant.

FURTHER EVIDENCE

Chapter Two discusses where water supplies come from and how water is collected and stored. What are the main points made in this chapter? What evidence is included to support these points? Read the article at the website below. Does the information on the website support the points made in the chapter? What new information does it present?

STORING AND MOVING WATER

abdocorelibrary.com/supplying-water

TREATING WATER

Water must meet quality standards before it is safe to use. The Safe Drinking Water Act (SDWA) is a federal law that was passed in 1974. This law protects the public by making sure drinking water is safe. The US Environmental Protection Agency (EPA) established water quality standards under the SDWA. These standards require that drinking water be tested for contaminants.

All water contains some level of contaminants. Contaminants include any matter found in water. Soil, pesticides, and

Water is thoroughly treated and cleaned inside water treatment plants.

Water passes through different tanks or basins as it's treated.

microbes are all contaminants. Contaminants can make
water look cloudy. They can make it smell and taste bad.
They can also make it dangerous to drink. The EPA is
concerned with contaminants that harm people's health.
It sets limits on more than 90 contaminants. In addition,
states may set their own water quality standards. Water
is treated at plants so that it is drinkable and usable.

FIRST STEPS

Water treatment steps may differ from one plant
to another depending on the technology available.
For example, some plants use UV treatment. This
treatment requires special technology and equipment.
Another factor affecting treatment steps is the quality

of the water. The water available in some areas may be cleaner than in other areas. It may not need to go through as many treatment steps. But most treatment plants follow similar steps.

Water that enters a treatment plant is held in large basins or tanks. In many plants, the water is first pumped through screens. Screens remove large items such as sticks and leaves. The next step is coagulation. Chemicals called coagulants are mixed into the water. Aluminum sulfate and ferric chloride are common coagulants. Coagulants act as magnets. They attract small particles such as sand and microbes. The particles bind with the coagulant. They form clumps called flocs.

After coagulation, the water flows into another basin. A machine stirs it. Stirring causes larger flocs to form. This step is called flocculation. The flocs sink to the bottom of the tank. These particles are then removed from the water.

FILTRATION AND DISINFECTION

After flocculation, the water is filtered. It is pumped into filter tanks. Filter tanks contain layers of sand, gravel, or charcoal. As the water moves down through the layers, the particles become trapped.

Then the water flows to a tank to be disinfected. Disinfectants such as chlorine or ozone gas are added into the tank. These substances kill viruses and bacteria that make people sick. The disinfectants also keep the water from picking up germs as it travels through pipes.

OZONE GENERATORS

Some facilities use ozone to disinfect water. Ozone is a molecule made of three oxygen atoms. The oxygen gas we breathe has two oxygen atoms. Ozone gas is produced inside an ozone generator. High-voltage electricity breaks up oxygen molecules inside a generator. The oxygen atoms reform as molecules of ozone. When ozone is pumped into water, it destroys harmful bacteria. It also removes pesticides. Ozone has the added benefit of improving the water's taste and smell.

In some plants, water goes through other types of treatment. Some plants use UV treatment. Some plants may add lime to the water to make it less acidic. Acids can weaken or destroy pipes. After the water has been completely treated, it is safe to drink and use. Then it is ready to be distributed.

DESALINATION PLANTS

Some treatment plants take in seawater. These are called desalination

Desalination plants extract saltwater from seas or oceans and treat it in large tanks.

plants. They remove salt and other minerals. This makes the water drinkable. Salt water is pumped through intake pipes from a nearby ocean or body of water to the plant. Some desalination plants heat water until it boils. The water evaporates into gas. The salt is left behind. Cold water pumped through coils cools the gas. The gas then turns back into water. Other plants use a process called reverse osmosis. Water is pumped through a filter. The filter catches salt and other small particles. Many people hope desalination plants will help provide water to regions prone to drought. But today's desalination processes use a lot of energy. They will need to become more efficient to be an environmentally friendly solution for dry regions.

WASTEWATER TREATMENT

Clean water is used in households and businesses. Then it flows down drains and into pipes. It enters the city's sewer system. A sewer system is made up of underground pipes. The pipes carry water to a wastewater treatment plant. At this plant, the wastewater is treated. Filters remove particles in the water. Bacteria break down organic matter. Then chlorine is added to kill bacteria. Other chemicals may be used to neutralize the chlorine, or make it ineffective. This is necessary because chlorine can harm fish and other marine life. The clean water then flows through pipes into an ocean or nearby river.

STRAIGHT TO THE
SOURCE

The Ogallala Aquifer stretches across the central United States. This water supply is being drained too quickly. Keith Gido, a professor of conservation biology at Kansas State University, described how this has affected the environment:

> *Large streams are more likely to be small. Everything has changed. We have almost completely changed the species of fish that can survive in those streams, compared with what was there historically. . . . It [aquifer draining] is happening all over the world in places such as Pakistan. It causes conflicts. As human populations grow, the demand for water is going to be greater. Conflicts are going to increase—unless we become more efficient in using the water we have.*

> Source: Brian Finley. "The Water under Colorado's Eastern Plains Is Running Dry as Farmers Keep Irrigating 'Great American Desert.'" *The Denver Post*. The Denver Post, October 8, 2017. Web. Accessed February 5, 2018.

Back It Up

The author of this passage is using evidence to support a point. Write a paragraph describing the point the author is making. Then list two or three pieces of evidence the author uses to make the point.

CHAPTER
FOUR

DISTRIBUTING WATER

After water has been treated, it is ready to be distributed. A large pipe carries water out of the plant. The water flows through the pipe to a pumping station. Pumps in the station push the water upward into aboveground storage tanks.

Water is stored in reservoirs, tanks, or towers. Water tanks and towers are made from concrete or steel. Engineers design storage tanks and towers to hold a day's worth of water. Reservoirs, tanks, or towers hold water in case of emergencies such as fires. Water is also stored so there will be enough available during peak demand times.

Water towers store treated water, which travels through pipes to a city's residents.

THE URBAN WATER CYCLE

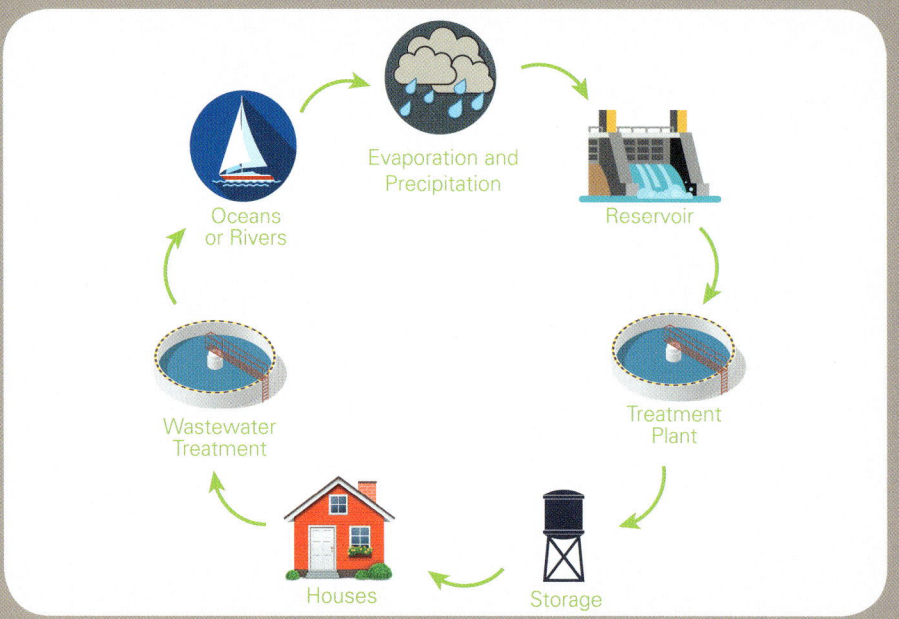

Evaporation and Precipitation

Oceans or Rivers

Reservoir

Wastewater Treatment

Treatment Plant

Houses

Storage

The above diagram shows how the water cycle works in an urban environment. Does this diagram help you better understand how water is collected and distributed in a community?

During peak demand, water usage is at its highest. Summers, mornings, and evenings are common peak demand times.

Water tanks are located at high elevations. Elevating a storage tank helps maintain constant water pressure. Many communities also build tall water towers. Gravity pushes down on the water inside the tank. The pressure pushes the water out of the tank and into attached pipelines. Extra water pressure is required to get water to the highest floors of tall buildings. Many buildings have their own pumps to do this job. Water is then stored in rooftop water towers.

MOVING WATER

Water moves from storage tanks to a community through pipes called water mains. Water mains are buried approximately 3 to 6 feet (1 to 2 m) below ground. This keeps the pipes from freezing in winter. It also protects the pipes from the weight of street-level traffic.

Pipes are built to withstand pressure from water flow. They also need to bear pressure caused by soil, aboveground traffic, and other loads. Engineers consider the force of water and other pressures when they build water supply pipes. Strong, wide pipes can best handle a heavy flow of water. Pipes may be made of concrete, iron, steel, or other strong materials.

Water mains branch off into smaller pipes called service lines. Service lines connect water mains to homes, businesses, and other buildings. In a city, water mains and service lines are usually looped together in a grid pattern. This ensures that water can flow to an area from more than one direction. If a break occurs in a line, the flow of water isn't halted. Water can still flow to buildings from another line.

As water enters a building, it passes through a water meter. The meter tracks how much water is used in each building. The owner of the building pays a fee based on the total volume of water that is used each month.

Water pipes connect to outlets within a building, such as faucets. Valves inside faucets hold back the water. Faucets can be turned on by lifting or turning a handle, such as a handle on a sink. Turning on a faucet opens a valve. Then water flows out.

Water meters measure how much water flows through a building's pipes.

Water is used in many ways. It is needed to wash dishes and clothes. Each load of laundry requires approximately 25 gallons (95 L) of water. Older laundry machine models may require more. People also use water to shower and keep clean. Showering may use up to 5 gallons (19 L) of water per minute. People depend on water for these tasks every day.

INFRASTRUCTURE REPORT CARD

In 2017 the American Society of Civil Engineers (ASCE) issued a report card for US water infrastructure. Drinking water infrastructure received a "D" grade. Wastewater infrastructure received a D+. Why such poor grades? According to the ASCE, nearly 6 billion gallons (23 billion L) of clean water are wasted in the United States each day because of leaky pipes. There are approximately 240,000 water main breaks each year. The ASCE estimates that more than 56 million new users will be added to US water systems within the next 20 years. Approximately $1 trillion will be needed to meet these demands over the next 25 years.

FIXING THE WATER SYSTEM

Much of the country's water supply infrastructure is in poor shape. Water mains in some US cities are more than 100 years old. Sewage collection pipes are often in disrepair. Pipes corrode, or break down, over time. Many pipes in older cities and towns are leaky. Shifting soil, freezing, and thawing put pressure on pipes. This can cause pipes to crack or break.

Cracked and leaky pipes waste water. Cracks also provide places for bacteria and chemicals to enter the water system. Cracked sewage pipes can leak contaminants into groundwater.

Repairing and replacing pipes is expensive. Many cities and towns cannot afford to upgrade their systems. The high cost keeps many cities from fixing infrastructure problems. Government officials are investigating ways

THE FLINT WATER CRISIS

Officials in Flint, Michigan, switched the city's source of drinking water in 2014. The new water supply came from the Flint River. But the water was not properly treated. It contained high amounts of chloride, a chemical that began to break down old lead pipes in the water supply system. The water became contaminated with lead. Exposure to lead is dangerous. It can affect brain development and cause other health problems. In response, the state provided free filters and water testing kits to Flint residents. Officials changed Flint's water supply source. The city has begun to replace aging lead service pipes. These steps are helping to solve Flint's water crisis.

to invest the money needed to improve the nation's water infrastructure.

The world's population is estimated to grow to 9.8 billion people by 2050. More water resources are used as the population increases. Water supply systems will need to be developed and improved to meet these demands. The EPA and other organizations are working together to solve water infrastructure issues. Engineers and scientists continue to develop new methods and technologies to collect, store, and distribute water. New technologies improve how water is monitored, cleaned, conserved, and delivered. Researchers are designing water infrastructure that may keep water safe and available for generations to come.

STRAIGHT TO THE
SOURCE

In 2017 a research team at the Massachusetts Institute of Technology (MIT) developed a robot that can detect leaks in pipes. Writer David L. Chandler reported on the new technology:

> *The system uses a small, rubbery robotic device. . . . The device can be inserted into the water system through any fire hydrant. It then moves passively with the flow, logging its position as it goes. It detects even small variations in pressure by sensing the pull at the edges of its soft rubber skirt, which fills the diameter of the pipe.*
>
> *The device is then retrieved using a net through another hydrant, and its data is uploaded. No digging is required, and there is no need for any interruption of the water service.*
>
> Source: David L. Chandler. "Finding Leaks While They're Easy to Fix." *MIT News*. MIT News, July 17, 2017. Web. Accessed February 5, 2018.

What's the Big Idea?
Read this passage carefully. What do you think are the benefits of this technology? How could it be used to maintain the water supply infrastructure?

FAST FACTS

- Americans use approximately 42 billion gallons (159 billion L) of water each day.

- Water is collected and stored using dams and reservoirs.

- At a water treatment plant, water is treated in several steps. This process removes contaminants so the water is safe to drink and use.

- Treated water is stored in reservoirs, tanks, or towers.

- Gravity moves water from water towers into pipes called water mains.

- Water mains branch off into smaller pipes called service lines. Service lines lead into homes, businesses, and other buildings.

- Usable water flows through faucets. People use this water for many tasks, such as showering.

- Used water flows down drains and into a sewer system. Pipes in the sewer system carry used water to wastewater treatment plants. Water is cleaned in these plants and fed back into rivers or oceans.

- The US water supply infrastructure is aging. Pipes and other infrastructure need to be repaired or replaced.

STOP AND
THINK

Tell the Tale

Chapter Three talks about how water is treated to make it safe to drink and use. Imagine you are touring a water treatment plant. Write 200 words describing the treatment process. What do you see? What steps are used to clean the water? Use lots of details to tell what is going on at the treatment plant.

Dig Deeper

After reading this book, what questions do you still have about supplying water to a city? With an adult's help, find a few reliable sources that can help you answer your questions. Write a paragraph about what you learned.

Say What?

Studying how water is supplied to a city can mean learning a lot of new vocabulary. Find five words in this book you've never heard before. Use a dictionary to find out what they mean. Then write the meanings in your own words, and use each word in a new sentence.

Why Do I Care?

Maybe you have never seen or visited a water treatment plant. But that doesn't mean you can't think about how important they are. How do you use water every day? How might your life be different if you lived somewhere without a modern water supply system or reliable access to water?

GLOSSARY

atom
a basic unit of an element

buoy
a floating object that is
anchored in place

canal
an artificial passage or
channel through which
water flows

conserve
to protect and
preserve something

hydraulic
having to do with water

infrastructure
the structures and systems a
city needs to run

microbe
a germ or other small
living organism

molecule
a substance made up of one
or more atoms

organic
something that comes from a
living organism

pesticide
a substance that is used to
kill insects and other pests

sensor
a device that responds to
aspects of the environment,
such as light or heat, and
collects data

watershed
a high area of land from
which streams or rivers drain
into a body of water

ONLINE RESOURCES

To learn more about supplying water for a city, visit our free resource websites below.

Visit **abdocorelibrary.com** for free Common Core resources for teachers and students, including vetted activities, multimedia, and booklinks, for deeper subject comprehension.

Visit **abdobooklinks.com** for free additional online weblinks for further learning. These links are routinely monitored and updated to provide the most current information available.

LEARN MORE

Bright, Michael. *From Raindrop to Tap.* New York: Crabtree Publishing, 2017.

Latham, Donna. *Canals and Dams: Investigate Feats of Engineering.* White River Junction, VT: Nomad Press, 2013.

INDEX

About the Author

Cecilia Pinto McCarthy has written several children's books about science and nature. She also teaches classes at a nature sanctuary. She and her family live north of Boston, Massachusetts.